❧ EX LIBRIS ❧

Compiled by Christopher Morley

[*"The most important autograph
in a book, is Your Own"*]

EX LIBRIS

("*The most important autograph
in a book, is Your Own*")

A small Anthology, printed and bound
(and sold) at the *First National Book
Fair* sponsored by the NEW YORK TIMES
and The National Association of Book
Publishers. Compiled at their request by

CHRISTOPHER MORLEY

NEW YORK CITY: NOVEMBER
1936

Note

EX LIBRIS was printed and published for the
New York Times First National Book Fair at
the Book Manufacturing Exhibit of the Book
Manufacturers' Institute, held at Rockefeller
Center, New York, November the 5*th* to 19*th*.
The Typography is by Richard W. Ellis of The
Haddon Craftsmen, Camden, New Jersey; the
Binding designed by Ernst Reichl of H. Wolff
Book Manufacturing Company, New York; and
the Jacket designed by Georg Salter, New York.

THIS LITTLE SCRAPBOOK

was put together during several rainy days, to be printed as a souvenir of the *First National Book Fair* in November 1936, a festival sponsored by the *New York Times* and the National Association of Book Publishers. I have purposely avoided the famous golden texts and purple passages of the bibliophile's evangel. You will not find Emily Dickinson's *There is no frigate like a book*, nor Wordsworth's *Books are a substantial world*, etc.; not even the well-loved but now too familiar rubrics from Lamb, Hazlitt, Leigh Hunt, Stevenson, Gissing and the others. Most of the fragments here are contemporary, and it was the editor's pleasure to choose not only "literary" bits but also odds and ends of trade and technical palaver.

The extracts are marked by numbers; each is duly identified in an index at the back. It will sometimes give the reader a pleasant surprise to find the authorship different from expectation.

Christopher Morley

October, 1936

EX LIBRIS

Compiled by Christopher Morley

1

Books are now multiplied to such a degree, that it is impossible not only to read them all, but even to know their number and their titles. Happily, one is not obliged to read all that is published.

2

There are readers—and I am one of them—whose reading is rather like a series of intoxications. We fall in love with a book; it is our book, we feel, for life; we shall not need another. We cram-throat our friends with it in the cruellest fashion; make it a Gospel, which we preach in a spirit of propaganda and indignation, putting a woe on the world for a neglect of which last week we were equally guilty.

3

The beauty of being a bookseller is that you don't have to be a literary critic: all you have to do to books is enjoy them. A literary critic is the kind of fellow who will tell you that Wordsworth's *Happy Warrior* is a poem of 85 lines composed entirely of two sentences—one 26 lines long and the other 59.

4

On a certain shelf in the bookcase are collected a number of volumes which look somewhat the worse for wear. Those of them which originally possessed gilding have had it fingered off, each of them has leaves turned down, and they open of themselves at places wherein I have been happy; each of them has remarks relevant and irrelevant scribbled on their margins. These favorite volumes cannot be called peculiar glories of literature; but out of the world of books have I singled them, as I have singled my intimates out of the world of men.

5

Unmitigated seriousness is always out of place in human affairs. Let not the unwary reader think me flippant for saying so; it was Plato, in his solemn old age, who said it.

6

We commonly see the booke that at Christmas lyeth bound on the Stationers stall, at Easter to be broken in the Haberdasshers shop.

7

In the hour after dinner, unless that had been a state affair, Napoleon used to glance over new books, throwing those which did not interest him upon the floor or into the fire. When on the road, it was the Emperor's usual practice to pitch ephemeral literature, and books which did not please him, out of the windows of his carriage. This explains why not infrequently books bearing his arms are to be found advertised in sale catalogues of London and Paris booksellers.

8

The right book at the right time may mean more in a person's life than anything else.

9

How uncomprehendingly must an angel from heaven smile on a poor human sitting engrossed in a romance: angled upon his hams, motionless in his chair, spectacles on nose, his two feet as close together as the flukes of a merman's tail, only his strange eyes stirring in his timeworn face.

SUZAN ELIZABETH, or *Life Begins at* 6:05 a.m. Evanston, Ill., October 22, 1935. Small, less than 1 mo. Good, clean copy. Weighs 7 lbs., 10 oz.

First edition, privately issued.

(The author collaborated with R. L. Brown in the first stages of this work.)

Conventional form, size and layout. Author's imprint on face. Natural make-up. In two colors, white and pink. Rubbed, shaken, unfoxed. Star border. Self cover when first issued, later with white wrappers on usual parts. Remarkably fine map in front. Appendix included. Rare in this untrimmed state.

11

The sales of this book were conceived in anaemia, born in pallor and seem destined to die of unbelievable indifference.

12

The good critic is he who describes the adventures of his soul among masterpieces.

13

The test of real fame in literature is to be reprinted in the *Old Farmer's Almanac*.

14

There are dynamite and wildcats in the prenatal life of a book. Any word as you see it here was first dipped up from a bottle of Stafford's Jet Black, then hammered out again through a typewriter ribbon, then punched in type on slivers of hot lead. It lived for a while on long galley sheets and was murmured, for syntax only, not for æsthetic ecstasy, in the patient sing-song of the proofreader. It was rammed into soft wax, went bathing in acid, drew to itself sparkling wraith-atoms of copper, strengthened itself for the world (as any idealist must) with heavy backing of alloy, lay down on the bed of a press, was run over by rollers of ink and crushed by huge sheets of paper. How alive they are, those presses! They gesticulate to you. Through the windows you see the white sheets flap to and fro. It is like prisoners waving shirts or kerchiefs to attract attention. Someone's words are there, impatient for life.

15

Someone should write a piece on the pleasures of book-buying these days when so many treasures can be had miracle cheap. It's nonsense to pull a long face about Depressions; they are pure felicity for the genuine booklover.

16

The greatest moment in my life as a publisher was when I opened the sheaf of manuscript that was *Last Poems* [by A. E. Housman]. I will go further and say that no publisher alive has had a greater thrill.

17

Three or four years ago we made a suggestion to the Poetry Society of America to the effect that it would be a good idea for poets and editors and publishers to abstain from producing and printing any poetry for the space of five years. We wished to see if the tone of the national life would not be perceptibly raised at the end of that time. But the plan was received with silence.

18

One cannot begin too soon to buy one's own books, if for no other reason (and there are many more) than the freedom which they give you to use their fly-leaves for your own private index of those matters in their pages which are particularly yours, whether for interest, or information, or what not— those things which the index-makers never by any possibility include. To be able to turn at will, in a book of your own, to those passages which count for you, is to have your wealth at instant command, and your books become a record of your intellectual adventures.

19

What other trade is there in the world so many-sided, with the power to engage so many different faculties and to perform so many different services to mankind?

20

The way we can tell whether we really like a book is, do we find ourself writing our name in it.

Be bold, be bold . . . but not too bold; among
new books buy something old. Chaucer, Shakespeare, Keats, and Blake, perfect Christmas pres-
ents make. Donne, Walt Whitman, Lamb, Mon-
taigne, these will help to keep you sane. And the
sun will ne'er go down, on those who read Sir
Thomas Browne. For a dish that's spiced and
mincy, try A. France or T. De Quincey. Then catch
up, a little later, with Melville, Coleridge, and
Pater. Beerbohm, Conrad, Conan Doyle, are goods
that Time is loth to spoil. O. Henry, Kipling, Oliver
Holmes, give you amperes and not ohms. Yea, ho-
sanna, these and others, gave their sisters and their
brothers, Words of life . . . so while you're at it
you'd Better think a Christmas gratitude.

Make *the* Works
Do not go into criticisms or arguments at all
Make full-blooded, rich, flush, natural Works
Insert natural things, indestructibles, idioms,
    characteristics, rivers, States, persons &c.
Be full of *strong sensual germs*

23

The fate of all Bookes depends upon your capacities: and not of your heads alone, but of your purses. Well, it is now publique, and you will stand for your privileges we know: to read, and censure. Do so, but buy it first. That doth best commend a Booke, the Stationer says.

24

To one whose business is with books there can be nothing more alluring than the contemplation at very close range of that astonishing phenomenon by which we all live—the Public. A course of salesmanship in a bookshop would modify that austere attitude of many authors toward their publishers and the distributors of their books who, it appears upon investigation, have virtues of their own, and difficulties which do not confront the authors.

25

I have never known persons who exposed themselves for years to constant interruption who did not muddle away their intellects by it at last.

Interruption is an evil to the reader which must be estimated very differently from ordinary business interruptions. The great question about interruption is not whether it compels you to divert your attention to other facts, but whether it compels you to tune your whole mind to another diapason. . . . If you are reading in the daytime in a house where there are women and children, or where people can fasten upon you for pottering details of business, you may be sure that you will *not* be able to get to the end of the passage without in some way or other being rudely awakened from your dream, and suddenly brought back into the common world. The loss intellectually is greater than anyone who had not suffered from it could imagine.

The world, you must remember, is only just becoming literate. As reading becomes more and more habitual and widespread, an ever-increasing number of people will discover that books will give them all the pleasures of social life and none of its intolerable tedium.

For three years I was a managing director in a big brewery. I have no sort of quarrel with brewing. It is an admirable trade, and beer is an admirable drink. But I have never been so bored in my life as I was during those three years. I learned then the lesson that nothing is so depressing as to spend one's life doing something in which one is not interested. Most of us would rather be making a competence out of books than a fortune out of soap.

Eugene Field's favorite haunt was the rare book department of McClurg's store. To this trysting place he gave the name of the Saints' and Sinners' Corner because of the bookmen who there convened about half were clergymen and the rest mostly newspaper men and actors. . . . There would be little piles of books on which Field would place a scrap of paper exhorting his good friends

> "For Jesus' sake forbear
> To buy the books assorted here,
> For what when I do get ye pelf
> I mean to buy ye same myself."

The more furiously and prodigiously books are put
in circulation, the more fluently will they pass into
the arteries of the second-hand trade; this is where
the real glamour of books has its color and essence.
In those dim aisles of dusty brethren, books come
to their just level. Their sins and sorrows are upon
them; they are no longer bricks of merchandize but
human emanations of triumph or disappointment.
They are no longer merely property; they become
audible as a voice from another world.

BOOK-OF-THE-MONTH, 1663

Dec. 26. Falling into a discourse of a new book
called *Hudibras*, I would needs go find it out, and
met with it at the Temple: cost me 2s 6d. But when
I came to read it, it is so silly that I am ashamed of
it; and by and by meeting at Mr. Townsend's at
dinner, I sold it to him for 18d.
Feb. 6. To a bookseller's in the Strand, and there
bought *Hudibras* again, it being certainly some ill
humour to be so against that which all the world
cries up.

TRYING TO SELL SOME SCOTCH
(Type, not Whiskey)

This Scotch Roman has been lying around for years in the shop where I work, and it depresses my amateur journalistic heart to see it idle, never having known the touch of printer's ink, when some young zealous journalist could make it serve its purpose, carrying thoughts from his eager pen to the printed page and out to the world to be read. These pounds and pounds of unused type are not needed in our plant because we have the same face on the machine. I wish I were a boy with a printing press and could get hold of the type I'm trying to sell—8, 10, and 12 point Scotch.

33

Sweet God, souse me in literature!

34

Digressions, incontestably, are the sunshine;—they are the life, the soul of reading!

35

The nice and subtle happiness of reading . . . .
this joy not dulled by age, this polite and unpun-
ished vice, this selfish, serene, life-long intoxication!

36

The Clarendon Press, known since 1830 as the Oxford University Press. In 1711-13 a new printing
house was erected for it by Sir John Vanbrugh. . . .
The name came from the funds being provided by
Lord Clarendon's *History of the Rebellion*, the
perpetual copyright of which was given to Oxford
University by his son.

37

In literature the language relationship made us
subject especially to England. The whole of the
nineteenth century was one long struggle to throw
off that domination—a struggle more or less suc-
cessful, but complicated in these later years by the
endless line of lionizing lecture tours of English
authors and by the attempt to control our culture
by the Rhodes Scholarships.

It is folly to assert that the literature of any nation or age was ever injured by plain speaking on the part of the critics. As for American Letters, plain speaking is the one thing needed. They are in a condition of absolute quagmire. . . . Perhaps Barrow is right after all, and the dearth of genius in America *is* owing to the continual teasing of the mosquitoes.

39

John Quinn, as you know, was a famous book collector. He owned the manuscript of *Ulysses*, I understand, and it is certain that he owned the manuscript of *The Crock of Gold*. (And here let me insert a warning. John Quinn at that time was hale and hearty. He enjoyed life, presumably, and he evidently enjoyed collecting books. Then he decided to sell his library, and he did so. *In less than a year* he was dead. I am not a psychologist, but as an observer of human nature I want to point out the danger of giving up an avocation. I warn all of you not to sell your books, and I urge you all to buy books so that you can enjoy the extra vitality of that "life beyond life.")

THE "MARBLED PAGE" IN
TRISTRAM SHANDY

Marbling of paper and book edges, as not everyone is aware, is done by spattering colors which float upon a liquid surface composed of gum and water where they may be manipulated in an infinity of patterns. The sheet of paper is gently laid upon this surface and taken up again with the colors adhering to it. In this manner the art has been practiced for several centuries.

Obviously this problem called for some form of mat which would mask out the margins and permit the color to touch only the rectangle of the page itself. To repeat this operation successfully some fifteen hundred times presented practical difficulties of a kind which I promise not to tell you about. It is enough to say that after many futile attempts to find the right thing, I finally constructed an affair of wood, with a mat of very flat sheet metal which holds the signatures of the book to guides for correct register, exposing a blank page through the opening in the mat. The whole thing is laid very carefully — to avoid air pockets which would cause blank spaces — upon the surface of floating color in a tank especially made for the purpose. It is taken up again with the color film adhering to its entire surface, but reaching the paper only through the opening in the mat. The excess liquid is drained off, the sheets removed, blotted, and then placed between blotters for drying. The surface of the tank must be wiped clean of remaining color by sliding strips of absorbent paper over it, a new pattern of color spattered on with small brooms made for the purpose, and the whole process repeated for another page.

Just as I often walk through lonely woods in Sussex to gather, wherever I see their golden gleam, certain funguses which are delicious eating, thus in the unfrequented thickets of old theology I collect words and phrases. Nor from any writings have I stolen more than from those of that master of verbal magic, Jeremy Taylor.

42

BACTERIUM BIBLIOPHILE

The micro-organism of booklore is a more active germ than some sentimentalists suppose. Although it is one of the oldest and proudest subdivisions of the disease of thinking, it is the least snobbish: it accepts all genuine devotees on equal terms. And it is not concerned only with desiderated states, primary editions, or inlaid bindings. It must be shrewd to discern the tincture of genius even in the most unlikely format. I have small respect for the bibliophile who only raves about established excellences —such as Voltaire, let us say—and cannot recognize on the hodiernal woodpulp paper the same spirit in Don Marquis or Westbrook Pegler.

43

One day when we were playing golf at St. Andrews, Mr. Carnegie turned to me and asked in his modest Scotch way: "How much money did you make in your book business last month?"

I told him I could not tell—that no publisher made up his books more than once a year, and it was impossible to figure the profit month by month.

He said: "Do you know what I would do if I were in a business in which I couldn't tell the amount of monthly profit?"

"No," I replied; "what would you do?"

"I would get out of it," he said.

This remark made a great impression on me and had a great effect on our business. We immediately set to work to organize our accounting department so that we could tell our condition at the end of each month.

44

It is beyond me to write of the vision I have always had at the base of my brain of the extent to which a publishing business could be carried in moral influence as well as in volume.

Literature is no easy emulsion. It requires, and opens itself only upon evidence of, the most brilliant and practised attention. The extenuated subtleties of its skill are incomparably diverse. If we knew precisely why a skilful writer uses one word rather than another (and he always does) we would know much more about the history of literature.

46
READING UPSIDE DOWN

His mother was an avid reader. . . . An amusing anecdote connected with Mrs. Firkins' reading habit concerns the appearance of *Uncle Tom's Cabin* in a newspaper (it must have been 1850 or near it). In her uncle's house, where the notion of a child perusing such frivolous matter was the typical one of the time, her frugal aunt pasted the issues of the newspaper containing the American classic on her kitchen walls—and upside down at that! Yet the girl developed a technique that enabled her to read the great story under that handicap. Lovers of literature were not pap-fed in those stern elder days.

47

Two stories I want awfully to get at are these: one
a hard, cruel theme of frustration (set perhaps in
Linotype Bodoni) and the other a light and fanci-
ful and beautiful thing (set, maybe, in French
Cochin).

48

It was the printing press that decided it: the greatest engine in the world, to which submarines and
howitzers and airplanes are but wasteful toys. For
when the printing presses are united the planet
may buck and yaw, but she comes into line at last.
A million inky cylinders, roaring in chorus, were
telling him the truth. . . .

For little by little the printed word incarnates
itself in power, and in ways undreamed of makes
itself felt. Little by little the wills of common men,
coalescing, running together like beads of mercury
on a plate, quivering into rhythm and concord, become a mighty force that may be ever so impalpable
but grinds empires to powder. Mankind suffers
hideous wrongs and cruel setbacks, but when once
the collective purpose of humanity is summoned,
it moves onward like the tide up a harbor.

49

He [the artist] speaks to our capacity for delight
and wonder, to the sense of mystery surrounding
our lives: to our sense of pity, and beauty, and pain:
to the latent feeling of fellowship with all creation
—and to the subtle but invincible conviction of
solidarity that knits together the loneliness of in-
numerable hearts . . . . which binds together all
humanity—the dead to the living and the living
to the unborn.

50

THE FIVE MILLION ELITE

Pareto did not want his book to be known to the
general public, since he felt that certain truths which
history reveals can do more harm than good if they
are known to the plain man, though knowledge of
them he regarded as essential to those who are or
who may one day be in or near the seats of power.
Pareto therefore addressed his book to the ruling
class of the western world, and in America this
means that the book is addressed to the five million people, who, it is said, constitute the intellectual elite.

The book clerk is in the position to remark certain human phenomena . . . most curious among them a pleasant hypocrisy. "Oh!" purls a sweet lady, pausing to glance for the space of a second at her surroundings, "I think books are just fine!" "I love to be in a book store," rattles a vivacious young woman. "Books have the greatest fascination for me," says another. A young lady waiting for friends looks out of the front door the entire time. Her friends express regret at having kept her waiting. "Oh!" she exclaims, "I have been so happy here" —glancing quickly around at the books—"I should just like to be left here a couple of years." There is a respectful pause by all for an instant, each bringing into her face an expression of adoration for the dear things of the mind. Then, chatting gaily, the party hastens away. We turn to hear, "Oh, wouldn't you love to *live* in a book shop!"

What is it that all men say in a book shop? The great say it, even, and the far from great. Each in his turn looks solemnly at his companion or at the salesman and says: "Of the making of books there is no end." Then each in his turn lights into a smile. He has said something pretty good.

"THE RIVET IN GRANDFATHER'S NECK"

Over the week-end Mr. Hodder had taken occasion to read for the first time Omar's *Rubaiyat*; also for the first time he had reviewed the art of Edmund Dulac. On that Monday morning, fresh from the exhausting exhilaration of an evangelically active Sabbath, he thrust himself into the office and presence of J.E.H.W. In his shaking hand he held a copy of Dulac's Omar Khayyam. This is the scene and the conversation as related to me by J.E.H.W. himself:

Mr. Hodder: "Ernest, what is this pagan book you have dared to publish over my imprint?"

J.E.H.W.: "Why, Grandad, that is one of the greatest classics of all time."

Mr. Hodder: "Classic or no classic, I will not tolerate the publication of such heathen rubbish."

J.E.H.W.: "Grandad, it is beautifully illustrated by one of the very greatest artists of our day—it is a proud production."

Mr. Hodder: "The artist only abets the author, whoever he is, in the presentation of a purely pagan and disgusting book. I will have none of it."

Driven into a corner by this Moses-like wrath of a modern patriarch, J.E.H.W. was at his wit's end for adequate defence. Finally he had the inspiration of three generations of commercial wisdom and quietly said, "But, Grandad, we made a profit of £800 on that book in the last twelve months." The violence of wrath subsided. Gradually a peaceful expression came over the old man's face—back came the benign and disarming smile. Patting his grandson gently on the shoulder, he admonished him, "You will be careful, Ernest, my boy, won't you?"

53

Here's the book I sought for so . . . .
    Let me see, let me see; is not the leaf turned down
Where I left reading? Here it is, I think.

54

I love to lose myself in a mystery.

55

The composition-imposition-makeready cost per copy of a certain book of 250 printed pages would be 84 cents, if the book were printed in an edition of only 500 copies; and the presswork would be 3½ cents per copy. However, if the edition was 10,000 copies, the composition-imposition-makeready cost would be only 4 cents; and the presswork would be a little more than 2 cents a copy. This accounts for the high prices of books which are printed in small quantities.

So far this year we have published 15 books. The average list price is $2.15. The average number of pages is 194. The average cost per page is $0.0111, which is close to the penny-a-page ideal.

56

They will ask him, "Do you take your characters from life?" How can he answer? He knows what they mean. They mean, "Did you lift such and such a character from an actual setting? Is it Mrs. This, or is it Dr. That?" Well, of course, it is not either. It is not an actual person, for how could an actual person fit into the covers of a book? The book is not a continent, not a definite geographical measure, it cannot contain so huge a thing as an actual full-size person. Any person has to be scaled by eliminations to fit the book world.

57

In reading some books we occupy ourselves chiefly with the thoughts of the author; in perusing others, exclusively with our own.

58

Not the sort of reading to be done slacked down in cushions, but set on a hard chair at a table with pencil handy—the way the best reading is done, alert, combative, fit to argue and consider.

ON THE RETURN OF A BOOK
LENT TO A FRIEND

I give hearty and humble thanks for the safe return of this book, which having endured the perils of my friend's bookcase and the bookcases of my friend's friends, now returns to me in reasonably good condition. I give hearty and humble thanks that my friend did not see fit to give this book to his infant for a plaything, nor use it as an ash tray for his burning cigar, nor as a teething-ring for his mastiff. When I loaned this book, I deemed it as lost; I was resigned to the business of the long parting; I never thought to look upon its pages again. But now that my book has come back to me, I rejoice and am exceedingly glad! Bring hither the fatted morocco and let us rebind the volume and set it on the shelf of honor, for this my book was lent and is returned again. Presently, therefore, I may return some of the books I myself have borrowed.

60

The condition of a writer's success as a writer—ignoring as long as we may his success as a manufacturer of seasonable novelties — is not timeliness. In fact it is the precise opposite of timeliness. The condition of any writer's success as an artist is the refusal to accept the fashionable esthetic dogmas of his time and the passion to establish a new and clean and unthumbed practice of his art. And the condition of any writer's success as an intelligence is the refusal to think as everyone about him thinks and the ceaseless effort to arrive at personal perceptions. In other words, a writer's real success is always founded in refusal to accept his time on its own terms. Quite commonly the time reciprocates.

61

A book, like a person, has its fortunes with one; is lucky or unlucky in the precise moment of its falling in our way, and often by some unhappy accident counts with us for something more than its independent value.

62

The Ancient Mariner would not have taken so well if it had been called *The Old Sailor*.

63

I would hardly go so far as to say that a book without an autograph, a bookplate, a thumb mark, a marginal note, a dog-ear, a slightly (but only slightly, please!) broken back, is but half a book. Yet there is something to be said for the notion that a book fresh from the press or the publisher's shelf is like a feast uneaten, a wine untasted, a colt unbroken, a talent unused. Such a book is too virginal for any but a furtive and frigid bibliotaph. For me, I prefer "good, second-hand condition" — with preferably a few stains of varied sorts, and a scribbled comment or two by a learned or a ribald owner. Such a book has at some time found a friend and been welcomed to someone's hearth.

64

Twenty-two acknowledged Concubines and a library of 62,000 volumes attested the variety of his inclinations; and from the products which he left behind him, it appears that the former as well as the latter were designed for use rather than ostentation.

65

Meek young men grow up in libraries, believing it their duty to accept the views which Cicero, which Locke, which Bacon, have given, forgetful that Cicero, Locke and Bacon were only young men in libraries when they wrote these books.

Hence, instead of Man Thinking, we have the bookworm. Hence, the book-learned class, who value books as such. Hence, the restorers of readings, the emendators, the bibliomaniacs of all degrees.

I had better never see a book, than to be warped by its attraction clean out of my own orbit, and made a satellite instead of a system.

66

He said: "The trouble with all you people is that you are always trying to reproduce Jenson's letters, or John de Spira or some of those Venetian people. You are always going back three or four hundred years and trying to do over again what they did then. . . .

"Take your curves and streamline 'em. Make a line of letters so full of energy that it can't wait to get to the end of the measure. My God—these Lino machines that you tell me about—what kind of letters would *they* spit out if you left it to *them*? 1500 Venetian? Not!"

67

Castles in Spain free with every purchase.

68

We were talking of what it is that sells a book. Charles Darwin said he did not believe it was reviews or advertisements, but simply "being talked about" that sold a book.

QUALITIES OF A HISTORIAN

It is impossible, through reading alone, to interpret the past. Nor is emotion enough. The historian must have a third quality as well: some conception of how men who are not historians behave. He can only gain that conception through personal experience, and he can only use his personal experiences when he is a genius. In Gibbon, as in no other English historian, this tenuous circle was complete. He was a genius who read, dreamed, and also knew—knew by direct contact, a fragment of the rough stuff of society, and extended his knowledge through the ages.

70

Never buy a book you cannot pay for promptly.

71

Consider the Bookseller. You may have overlooked the dignity of his calling: the indispensable link between the productive brain and the eager mind.

72

How pleasant it is to respect people! When I see books, I am not concerned with how the authors loved or played cards; I see only their marvellous works.

73

One always tends to overpraise a long book, because one has got through it.

74

One of the best ways (perhaps the only way) to abash an Author is to let him see a book of his own actually running on the press. I saw a writer the other day watching sheets of his book printing on Miehle number 8 at the Country Life Press. It is a thrilling sight—those great sheets (32 pages on each side) flapping forward at you, running over a line of flame as they come—"to take the electricity out of it," said the pressman; but the author thought secretly, If there is any electricity in the book, better leave it there.

BED-BOOKS

There are a few books which go with midnight, solitude, and a candle. It is much easier to say what does not please us than what is exactly right. The book must be something benedictory by a sinning fellow man. Cleverness would be repellant at such an hour. Cleverness, anyhow, is the level of mediocrity today; we are all too infernally clever. The first witty and perverse paradox blows out the candle. Only the sick in mind crave cleverness. . . .

Though at that hour the body may be dog-tired, the mind is white and lucid, like that of a man from whom a fever has abated.

IDENTIFICATIONS

1. Voltaire: *Philosophical Dictionary*.
2. Logan Pearsall Smith:
   Reperusals and Re-Collections.
3. Roger Mifflin (*The Haunted Bookshop*).
4. Alexander Smith: *Dreamthorp*.
5. George Santayana: *Soliloquies in England*.
6. Lyly: preface to Euphues (1579).
7. James Westfall Thompson:
   Byways in Bookland.
8. Lee Shippey, in the Los Angeles Times.
9. Walter de la Mare.
10. Richard L. Brown, Chicago printer, on the birth of a daughter.
11. Letter from the Argus Bookshop, Chicago.
12. Anatole France: preface to *La Vie Litteraire*.
13. Arthur W. Bell.
14. *John Mistletoe*.
15. *The Bowling Green*.
16. Grant Richards: *Author Hunting*.
17. Don Marquis: *The Almost Perfect State*.

18. John Livingston Lowes: *Of Reading Books.*
19. Geoffrey Faber, Address to British Booksellers, 1931.
20. *Trade Winds.*
21. P. E. G. Quercus.
22. Walt Whitman: preliminary notes for *Leaves of Grass* (1855).
23. Heming and Condell: *To the Great Variety of Readers* in the First Folio Shakespeare, 1623.
24. William McFee: *The High Seas Bookshop*
25. Florence Nightingale: quoted by P. G. Hamerton, *The Intellectual Life.*
26. P. G. Hamerton, *ibid.* (*Letter to a Man of Business Who Desired to Make Himself Better Acquainted with Literature.*)
27. Aldous Huxley: *Crome Yellow.*
28. Geoffrey Faber, Address to British Booksellers, 1931.
29. Harry B. Smith: *First Nights and First Editions.*
30. *The Book Dial*, December 1923.

31. Pepys' Diary, 1662-63.

32. Advertisement of Helen Spink, printer in
    Louisville, Ky.

33. T. J. Cobden-Sanderson, the famous printer
    of the Doves Press. Used by Dana Jones as
    a bookplate motto.

34. Sterne: *Tristram Shandy*.

35. Logan Pearsall Smith: *Trivia*.

36. *Everyman's Encyclopaedia*.

37. Grant Wood: *Revolt Against the City*.

38. Edgar Allan Poe: *Marginalia*.

39. *Along the North Wall*, catalogue of Argus
    Bookshop, Chicago.

40. T. M. Cleland, describing his work on the
    Limited Editions Club issue of *Tristram
    Shandy*. The famous marbled page is in
    Book iii, chapter 36.

41. Logan Pearsall Smith:
    Reperusals and Re-Collections.

42. *The Bowling Green*.

43. Frank Nelson Doubleday:
    Some Indiscreet Recollections
    (privately printed, 1928).

44. Frank Nelson Doubleday: *Ibid.*

45. *The Eumenides of Book Collecting.*

46. Richard Burton: *Memoir of Oscar Firkins*
    (brilliant teacher and critic at the University of Minnesota; obit. 1932).

47. Letter from Robert O. Ballou.

48. *Shandygaff* (1918).

49. Joseph Conrad: preface to
    The Nigger of the Narcissus.

50. Harcourt Brace & Co., pamphlet announcing
    Pareto: *The Mind and Society*, 1935.

51. Robert Cortes Holliday: *Humors of the Book
    Shop* (in *Walking Stick Papers*).

52. George H. Doran: *Chronicles of Barabbas.*

53. Brutus, in *Julius Caesar*, Act IV, Scene 3.
    He and Alexander Smith both had the bad habit of dog's-earing.

54. Sir Thomas Browne: *Religio Medici*
(Part I, Section 8).

55. *The Pleasures of Publishing*, Columbia
University Press.

56. Pearl S. Buck: *Advice to Unborn Novelists*.

57. Edgar Allan Poe: *Marginalia*.

58. P. E. G. Quercus.

59. *The Haunted Bookshop*.

60. Archibald MacLeish: address to the National
Association of Book Publishers, 1935.

61. Walter Pater: *Marius the Epicurean*

62. *Notebooks of Samuel Butler*.

63. Carl P. Rollins, letter to the
Saturday Review of Literature.

64. Gibbon, of one of the Caesars. Quoted in
catalogue of Arthur Rogers, Newcastle-
on-Tyne.

65. Emerson: *The American Scholar* (1837).

66. W. A. Dwiggins: *On a New Linotype Face*
(1935).

67. Jake Zeitlin, bookseller, in his catalogue.

68. *Notebooks of Samuel Butler.*
69. E. M. Forster: *Abinger Harvest.*
70. A. Edward Newton: preface to Modern
    Library edition of *The Amenities of Book
    Collecting.*
71. Charles K. Stotlemeyer, bookseller of
    Hancock, Maryland.
72. Notebook of Anton Chekhov.
73. E. M. Forster: *Abinger Harvest.*
74. *The Bowling Green.*
75. H. M. Tomlinson:
    Bed-Books and Night-Lights.

About the Making of this Book

The printing of EX LIBRIS was done under the supervision of The Haddon Craftsmen, Camden, New Jersey; and the binding under the supervision of H. Wolff Book Manufacturing Company, New York. The jacket was printed in four-color Offset by The DeVinne-Brown Corporation, New York.

The Composition, in Linotype Electra, was by The Composing Room, Inc., New York; Paper, Glatfelter wove by Perkins & Squire Company, New York; the Binding cloth by Holliston Mills, New York; Binding Dies by the Truart Reproduction Company, New York; Gold Leaf by Peerless Roll Leaf Company, Union City, New Jersey.